MAKING FIRE
IN THE WILD

LOUELLA BATH

New York

Published in 2016 by The Rosen Publishing Group, Inc.
29 East 21st Street, New York, NY 10010

First Edition

Editor: Sarah Machajewski
Book Design: Michael J. Flynn

Photo Credits: Cover (man) Jupiterimages/Thinkstock.com; cover, pp. 1, 3–4, 6, 8–10, 12, 14–16, 18, 20, 22–24 (map background) Sergei Drozd/Shutterstock.com; pp. 4–5 (family hiking) oliveromg/Shutterstock.com; p. 7 Hero Images/DigitalVision/ Getty Images; p. 8 Olesia Bilkei/Shutterstock.com; p. 9 Charles Knowles/Shutterstock.com; p. 10 Andrew Scheck/Shutterstock.com; p. 11 (notepad background) stocksolutions/Shutterstock.com; p. 11 (canned food, water bottle, backpack, tent, flint, first-aid kit, compass, matches) zelimirz/Shutterstock.com; p. 11 (map) filip robert/Shutterstock.com; p. 11 (whistle) Finevector/Shutterstock.com; p. 11 (newspaper) softRobot/Shutterstock.com; p. 11 (magnifying glass) Victoria Chernous/Shutterstock.com; p. 13 Dutourdumonde Photography/Shutterstock.com; p. 14 Deyan Georgiev/Shutterstock.com; p. 15 amana productions inc/Getty Images; pp. 16–17 by Michael Flynn; p. 18 Pavel L Photo and Video/Shutterstock.com; p. 19 Lebazele/Shuterstock.com; p. 21 gorillaimages/Shutterstock.com; p. 22 Melissa E Dockstader/Shutterstock.com.

Cataloging-in-Publication Data

Bath, Louella.
Making fire in the wild / by Louella Bath.
p. cm. — (Wilderness survival skills)
Includes index.
ISBN 978-1-5081-4320-8 (pbk.)
ISBN 978-1-5081-4316-1 (6-pack)
ISBN 978-1-5081-4321-5 (library binding)
1. Wilderness survival — Juvenile literature. 2. Fire — Juvenile literature. I. Bath, Louella. II. Title.
GV200.5 B38 2016
613.6'9—d23

Manufactured in the United States of America

CPSIA Compliance Information: Batch #BW16PK: For Further Information contact Rosen Publishing, New York, New York at 1-800-237-9932

CONTENTS

A NOTE TO READERS

Always talk with a parent or teacher before proceeding with any of the activities found in this book. Some activities require adult supervision.

A NOTE TO PARENTS AND TEACHERS

GET OUTSIDE!

People love to spend time outdoors. Our planet has many **landscapes** for us to enjoy—from beautiful beaches to pretty forests. There are many great things to do in the **wilderness**, including hiking, camping, and having outdoor picnics.

The wilderness offers plenty of opportunities to have fun, but it's not without its **challenges**. It can pose major dangers to your health and safety. It's important to have survival skills that will help you face the wilderness head-on.

Even though it's fun to explore the wilderness, it's important to always be careful and prepared. You never know what may happen!

READY FOR ANYTHING

Part of being a wilderness adventurer is having survival skills. A survival skill is anything that helps you stay alive in a dangerous, or unsafe, **situation**. If you find yourself in a survival situation, your survival skills may be what keep you alive and healthy until you can reach safety. That's why they're so important.

Building **shelter**, making tools, and knowing how to locate food and water are important skills. This book will focus on how to make fire.

SURVIVAL TIP

Don't wait until you're in a survival situation to learn these important skills. Practice them before heading out into the wilderness.

Learning survival skills takes time and practice. Stick with it, and soon, you'll be prepared to survive in the wilderness.

LIGHT OF LIFE

Fire has been important to humans since the earliest **civilizations**. Once ancient people discovered how to make it, they had light and warmth they could control. They could cook food. They used fire's heat to help make tools and other objects. Fire also kept people safe.

Today, our uses for fire are much like those from long ago. When we're outside, fire keeps us warm. It helps us see in the wilderness, which gets really dark at night. It's also great for roasting marshmallows! And it's absolutely necessary in survival situations.

Knowing how to make fire is an important skill to have. It comes in handy whether you're making a campfire or a fire that will help you survive.

BEFORE YOU GO

Before you head into the wilderness, spend time preparing for your trip. Think about where you're going. What might you need while you're there? You'll probably pack food, water, and camping gear. Make sure to bring fire-starting supplies, too.

You'll use materials, or matter, from the wilderness to make your fire, but bring something to help you start it. A lighter or matches are good tools. You can also bring **tinder**, such as paper or dry wood. However, tinder can also be found around your campsite.

SURVIVAL TIP

Pack your matches or lighter in something that will keep them dry, such as a plastic holder.

PACKING LIST

FOOD

FIRST-AID KIT

COMPASS

WATER

(OR SUPPLIES TO MAKE IT CLEAN)

CAMPING GEAR

MATCHES OR A LIGHTER

(AND SOMETHING TO KEEP THEM DRY)

MAGNIFYING GLASS

WHISTLE

FLINT

(SEE PAGE 18)

TINDER

(SUCH AS NEWSPAPER OR DRYER LINT)

MAP

FIRE FORMULA

Fire needs three things to start and burn: heat, oxygen, and fuel. Heat comes from matches or another fire starter. Oxygen is a gas in the air. Fuel is something that burns to produce heat, such as wood. These three things are known as the "fire triangle."

Fires only continue to burn if all three parts of the triangle are present. If you take one away, the fire will go out. Keep the fire triangle in mind as you read about how to start a fire in the wilderness.

FIRE TRIANGLE

FUEL

OXYGEN

HEAT

On their own, heat, oxygen, and fuel may not seem like much. When you mix them together, they create something very important.

STARTING A FIRE WITH A MATCH

You've arrived at your campsite and set up your gear. Now it's time to make your fire. Look around your campsite for fuel, such as branches and logs. Gather smaller sticks to use as **kindling**. Finally, gather dry grass, leaves, and twigs to use as tinder.

Pile your kindling in the center of your fire. Place the larger pieces of wood in the shape of a tepee. Then, gather a handful of tinder. Light the tinder with a match. Place it under your kindling. The fire should soon spread to the tepee.

A tepee shape is when the logs meet at the top and spread out in a circle around the bottom.

If your fire seems like it's not catching, blow on its base. This adds oxygen and will help it spread to the bigger wood. However, be careful—this can cause the fire to flare up quickly.

NO MATCH? NO PROBLEM!

Wilderness adventurers must expect the unexpected. What happens if your matches get wet? You need to make fire another way.

Try using a hand drill. Gather a straight stick, tree bark, and a wooden board. Make a V-shaped cut along the board's edge. Place the bark under it. Make a hole at the tip of the V. Place the stick (also called the spindle) in the hole and rub it between your hands. The heat and **friction** of the stick rubbing against the board will produce an **ember**. Carefully move the ember to the bark, then use it to light your tinder.

SURVIVAL TIP

Hand drills and bow drills require a lot of time, so stick with them, even if they seem like they're not working.

A bow drill works a lot like a hand drill, but it may be easier. Instead of using your hands, you wrap the string of a bow around the spindle. Moving the bow back and forth turns the spindle and creates the friction needed to start a fire.

SPINDLE

BOW

You can create a spark with a flint and steel, such as the blade of a knife. Drag a knife along the flint until you see sparks. Or use a magnifying glass and the sun. Hold a magnifying glass above a pile of tinder, focusing a beam of sunlight through the lens. If the sunlight is strong enough, it will **ignite** the tinder after several minutes.

Another way to create a spark is to rub the top of a battery against **steel wool**. When the steel wool glows, blow on it gently to spread the ember.

These fire-starting methods may only produce a couple of sparks or embers. Make sure to have tinder ready. When you get a spark or ember, carefully use it to light the tinder. Then, use the tinder to light the fire.

USES FOR FIRE

How can you use fire? For an overnight trip, you'll use a campfire for light and warmth. It's fun to cook dinner over a campfire. It makes you feel like a true wilderness adventurer! Always remember to put your fire out before you fall asleep and before you leave your campsite.

If you're in a survival situation, fire is extremely important. It keeps you warm and may scare wild animals away. You can use it to cook food and boil water. Finally, you can use fire as a **signal**. If people are looking for you, they can spot a big fire from far away.

SURVIVAL TIP

If you need to be rescued, build three big fires. Three fires together is a sign someone needs help.

It's fun to sit around a campfire and share stories!

SAFETY FIRST!

Always be careful around fire. Only build it in a clear area, away from trees or tall grass. Surround your fire with a circle of rocks so it won't spread.

Never leave your fire unattended, and always put it out when you leave. You can pour water or sand on it, but make sure it's fully out—even embers can restart a fire. Don't let your body, clothes, or gear get too close to the fire. Following these tips will keep you—and nature—safe while you practice your survival skills.

GLOSSARY

challenge: Something that tests someone's abilities.

civilization: Organized society with written records and laws.

ember: A small piece of burning matter.

flint: A hard gray rock that can produce a spark when rubbed with steel.

friction: The force created when one object moves over another.

ignite: To catch fire.

kindling: Small twigs or sticks that are used for starting a fire.

landscape: The natural features of an area.

shelter: A place that keeps a person safe from bad weather.

signal: An action or sound used to show someone something. Also, to show someone something using an action or sound.

situation: A series of events in which a person finds themself.

steel wool: Fine strands of steel that are balled together.

tinder: Dry matter that can be used to light a fire.

wilderness: A natural, wild place.

INDEX

WEBSITES

Due to the changing nature of Internet links, PowerKids Press has developed an online list of websites related to the subject of this book. This site is updated regularly. Please use this link to access the list: www.powerkidslinks.com/wss/fire